Paleo Smoothies

Recipes To Energize and for Weight Loss

Introduction:

The Paleo diet is considered the world's healthiest diet. The diet is reminiscent of the hunter gatherer lifestyle that was prevalent 2.6 million years ago. The diet includes: fresh meat, eggs, fresh fruits and vegetables, nuts and seeds and also healthy oils (olive, walnut, flaxseed, macadamia, avocado and coconut oil). Grains, dairy products, and sugar are not part of the diet. The Paleo diet is said to help protect against obesity, cardiovascular disease, type 2 diabetes and many more. Overall the Paleo diet provides a strong lifestyle and is a healthy way to live.

Smoothies are an easy and fast way to follow the Paleo diet. With such a large variety of smoothies, it is easy to find a new smoothie to drink daily. They can be drunk for an easy breakfast or a quick snack. They can be drunk slowly or taken on the go. This book has recipes that are not only healthy but they also use common ingredients that one following the paleo diet should have readily available.

For many recipes in this cookbook, the ingredients are listed but there are no instructions on how to prepare the smoothie. The easiest way to prepare a smoothie is by combining all the ingredients into a blender and process until smooth. If your smoothie is too thick, add water. If your smoothie is too thin, add ice. If your smoothie is too bitter or sour, add a banana for extra sweetness. If you need an extra serving of vegetables, add a handful of spinach or kale.

Nutrition facts are listed with each smoothie recipe. These nutrition facts are based on a 2,000 calorie diet.

Disclaimer:

The information in this book is in no way intended as medical advice. The ideas and recipes should be used in combination with other sources to create a balanced diet. You should consult your physician before starting any diet and for any sort of Nutrition advice. The author disclaims responsibility for any adverse health effects that come in combination with the use of these recipes.

This book and all the recipes contained therein is the sole property of Angelina Dylon. Any copy or distribution of this work is prohibited.

Table of Contents

Vegetable Smoothies

Avocado almond smoothie

Serves 1

1 cup all natural Almond milk

1/4 cup Almonds

1/2 Banana

1/4 of an Avocado

Handful of Ice

Taste a savory, slightly sweet smoothie. To make a sweeter smoothie, add more bananas.

Nutrition facts: Serving size 373 g; Calories 347; Calories from Fat 218; Total Fat 24.2 g, 37 % DV; Saturated Fat 2.0 g 10% DV; Cholesterol 0 mg; Sodium 154 mg 6% DV; Sodium 154mg 6% DV; Total Carbohydrates 26.9 g 9% DV; Dietary Fiber 8.8 g 35% DV; Sugars 15.5 g; Protein 7.6g; Vitamin A 12%; Vitamin C 17%; Calcium 37%; Iron 9%

Spiced Pumpkin Smoothie

Serves 1

½ cup pumpkin

1 cup unsweetened almond milk

½ small banana, frozen

½ tablespoon Raw honey

½ teaspoon vanilla extract

¼ teaspoon cinnamon

1/8 teaspoon ginger

1/8 teaspoon nutmeg

1/8 teaspoon ground cloves

1/8 teaspoon allspice

Handful of ice

This smoothie is as good as a pumpkin pie! Enjoy this on Thanksgiving as a healthy substitute for pie.

Nutrition Facts: Serving Size 427 g; Calories 160; Calories from fat 29; Total Fat 3.2 g 5% DV; Cholesterol 0mg; Sodium 188 mg 8% DV; Total Carbohydrates 32.5 g 11% DV; Dietary Fiber 6.4 g 26 % DV; Sugars 19.2 g; Protein 3.0 g; Vitamin A 392%; Vitamin C 17%; Calcium 50%; Iron 15%

Pumpkin Blueberry Smoothie

Serves 2

1 cup pureed pumpkin

½ cup frozen blueberries

1 Banana

1 cup coconut milk

½ cup water

1 cup Spinach

½ teaspoon cinnamon

Nutrition Facts: Serving Size 340 g; Calories 354; Calories from fat 261; Total Fat 29.0 g 45% DV; Saturated Fat 25.5 g 127% DV; Cholesterol 0 mg; Sodium 33 mg 1% DV; Total Carbohydrates 26.4 g 9% DV; Dietary Fiber 5.7 g 23% DV; Sugars 14.9 g; Protein 4.1 g; Vitamin A 29%; Vitamin C 27%; Calcium 5%; Iron 15%

Apple and Blackberry Smoothies

Blackberry Cacao Smoothie

Serves 2

2 Bananas

1 cup blackberries

1 cup coconut milk

1 Apple, peeled

2 Tablespoon raw cacao

Nutrition Facts: Serving Size 310g; Calories 412; Calories from fat 264; Total Fat 29.3g 45% DV; Saturated Fat 25.5g 128% DV; Cholesterol 0mg; Sodium 20mg 1% DV; Total Carbohydrates 40.5g 14% DV; Dietary Fiber 9.5g 38% DV; Sugars 21.9g; Protein 5.0g; Vitamin A 5%; Vitamin C 48%; Calcium 5%; Iron 15%

Coconut milk vs. Almond milk

Adding a milk substitute to your smoothie not only adds nutrients but it also gives your smoothie a creamy texture.

Almond milk is an option that is low in calories. For a serving on unsweetened almond milk, it is only 30 calories (the sweetened, vanilla flavored is about 90 calories). Also it has a good amount of Magnesium, Potassium and Vitamin E.

Coconut milk, while it tastes good has a lot of calories, 550 calories per can. It also contains a lot of Saturated Fat. It is possible to buy a low calorie coconut milk or you can even buy a coconut and almond milk blend that is lower in calories.

Tomato Smoothies

Tomato Parsley Smoothie

Serves 3

3 cups tomatoes, Roma tomatoes are best

2 cups ice

1 cup flat-leaf parsley

1 cup water

1 medium avocado

3 Tbsp fresh lemon juice

3 tsp Olive oil

2 tsp finely chopped red onion

2 cloves minced garlic

1 tsp chopped sun-dried tomatoes

¾ tsp chopped Serrano chili

¾ tsp salt

Combine all ingredients in a blender and blend until smooth. Add more of the Serrano chili if you desire.

Nutrition Facts: Serving Size 500g; Calories 212; Calories from Fat 165; Total Fat 18.3g 28% DV; Saturated Fat 2.2g 11% DV; Cholesterol 0mg; Sodium 615mg 26% DV; Total Carbohydrates 8.6g 3% DV; Dietary Fiber 7.1g 28% DV; Sugars 4.9g; Protein 3.5g; Vitamin A 36%; Vitamin C 121%; Calcium 5%; Iron 23%

Tomato Carrot Smoothie

Serves 2

4 Carrots, peeled and cubed

6 tomatoes, chopped

Salt

1 stalk celery

1 pinch fresh ground pepper

1 fresh squeezed lemon

Freeze the tomatoes and carrots. Blend them together until smooth.

Nutrition Facts: Serving Size 500g; Calories 117; Calories from Fat 8; Total Fat 0.9g 1% DV; Cholesterol 0mg; Sodium 187 mg 8% DV; Total Carbohydrates 26.4g 9% DV; Dietary Fiber 8.1g 32% DV; Sugars 15.5g; Protein 4.5g; Vitamin A 410%; Vitamin C 142%; Calcium 5%; Iron 36%

Banana and Strawberry Smoothies

Strawberry, Banana, Orange smoothie

Serves 1

A sweet smoothie to brighten your morning!

6 juicy strawberries

1 orange

1 mango

1 cup water

 Handful of ice

1 frozen banana

Nutrition Facts: Serving Size 256g; Calories 111; Calories from fat 2; Total fat 0.2g 0% DV; Cholesterol 0mg; Sodium 0mg; Total Carbohydrates 27.0g 9% DV; Dietary Fiber 5.4g 22% DV; Sugars 21.1g; Protein 2.2g; Vitamin A 8%; Vitamin C 242%; Iron 2 %

Did you know?

Bananas that need to ripen should be left at room temperature, but away from direct heat and sun. Bananas that are perfectly ripe can stay ripe for 2-3 days longer if stored in the fridge. If you don't plan on using the banana, peel it, slice it up and place it in a baggie in the freezer to add to your smoothies another day.

Strawberry, Pineapple Smoothie

Serves 3

2 cups pineapple juice

2 cups strawberries

1 banana

1 cup diced peaches

Ice cubes

Blend the ingredients together until smooth.

Nutrition Facts: Serving Size 359g; Calories 178; Calories from Fat 4; Total Fat 0.5g 1% DV; Cholesterol 0mg; Sodium 4mg 0% DV; Total Carbohydrates 43.0g 14% DV; Dietary Fiber 3.5g 14% DV; Sugars 31.4g; Protein 2.2g; Vitamin A 4%; Vitamin C 144%; Calcium 4%; Iron 6%

Strawberry, Banana, Almond Smoothie

Serves 2

1 frozen banana

8 strawberries

2 Tablespoons almond butter

1 Cup Almond Milk

2 Cups Spinach

Nutrition Facts: Serving Size 203g; Calories 177; Calories from Fat 84; Total Fat 9.3g 14% DV; Saturated Fat 0.9g 5% DV; Cholesterol 0mg; Sodium 24mg 1% DV; Total Carbohydrates 21.0g 7% DV; Dietary Fiber 3.4g 14% DV; Sugars 10.0g; Protein 5.2g; Vitamin A 57%; Vitamin C 75%; Calcium 8%; Iron 9%

Berry, Banana Smoothie

Serves 2

1 cup Spinach

10 frozen Strawberries

½ cup frozen blueberries

1 cup coconut milk

1 teaspoon honey

1 Banana

Nutrition Facts: Serving Size 385g; Calories 413; Calories from Fat 261; Total Fat 29.0g 45% DV; Saturated Fat 25.5g 127% DV; Cholesterol 0mg; Sodium 31mg 1% DV; Total Carbohydrates 41.8g 14% DV; Dietary Fiber 8.4 g 34% DV; Sugars 26.7g; Protein 4.1g; Vitamin A 29%; Vitamin C 117%; Calcium 6%; Iron 19%

Strawberry, Mango Smoothie

Serves 2

1 Mango, peeled

1 cup frozen strawberries

1 banana

1 cup Almond milk

Ice

Nutrition Facts: Serving Size 716 g; Calories 350; Calories from Fat 35; Total Fat 3.9g 6% DV; Cholesterol 0mg; Sodium 155mg 6% DV; Total Carbohydrates 83.0g 28% DV; Dietary Fiber 11.1g 44% DV; Sugars 61.4g; Protein 3.4g; Vitamin A 44%; Vitamin C 203%; Calcium 50%; Iron 11%

Green Smoothies

Sweet and Green smoothie

Serves 1

1 cup frozen pineapple

1 pear

½ cup unsweetened vanilla almond milk

1 cucumber

2 cups kale

½ teaspoon of chia seeds

Blend all the ingredients together except for the chia seeds. Add the chia seeds after the ingredients are smooth and ready to drink.

Nutrition Facts: Serving Size 744g; Calories 291; Calories from Fat 70; Total Fat 7.7g 12% DV; Saturated Fat 0.7g 4% DV; Cholesterol 0mg; Sodium 155 mg 6% DV; Total Carbohydrates 52.1g 17% DV; Dietary Fiber 14.2g 57% DV; Sugars 14.1g; Protein 10.6g; Vitamin A 424%; Vitamin C 292%; Calcium 54%; Iron 33%

Why Chia Seeds?

Chia seeds have become increasingly more popular; they don't have a very strong taste and are easy to add to food. Chia seeds are high in Omega 3 and also high in dietary fiber. Omega-3is an essential fatty acid that is necessary in order for our body to function properly. Increased Omega-3 may even lower blood pressure and help with arthritis and depression. Dietary fiber is what helps the body stay fuller, longer thus preventing one from over indulging.

Green Pineapple smoothie

Serves 1

1 mango, peeled

2 cups kale

2 cups fresh pineapple

¼ avocado

1 small banana

2 kiwis, peeled

Handful of ice

This is a great smoothie for if you start to feel a little sick. It is packed with the Vitamin C that will help your immune system to fight whatever is bringing you down.

Nutrition Facts: Serving Size 437g; Calories 348; Calories from fat 107; Total Fat 11.9g 18% DV; Saturated Fat 1.3g 7% DV; Cholesterol 0mg; Sodium 67mg 3% DV; Total Carbohydrates 59.0g 20% DV; Dietary Fiber 13.2g 53% DV; Sugars 26.3g; Protein 8.2g; Vitamin A 417%; Vitamin C 526%; Calcium 24%; Iron 18%

Why Kale?

Kale is a power green. It is a simple green that is packed full of Vitamins A, C and K. In just one cup of kale you have 206% of your daily value of vitamin A, 134% of vitamin C, and 684% of vitamin K. Vitamin A is important in maintaining normal vision, it is also essential for healthy teeth, skeletal tissue and skin. Vitamin C is an antioxidant; it helps boost the immune system and is essential for the absorption of iron. Vitamin K is important in helping the blood clot which helps prevent excess bleeding. Vitamin K is also said to help increase bone density and aid in preventing cancer.

Spinach peach green smoothie

Serves 3-4

2 bananas

2 cups spinach

1 cup fresh pineapple or ½ can of pineapple

1 cup frozen peaches

1 ½ cups coconut milk

Serve this smoothie to the whole family for a delicious snack or for a great breakfast.

Nutrition Facts: Serving Size 275g; Calories 373; Calories from Fat 262; Total Fat 29.1 45% DV; Saturated Fat 25.5 127% DV; Cholesterol 0mg; Sodium 35mg 1% DV; Total Carbohydrates 30.0g 10% DV; Dietary Fiber 6.0g 24% DV; Sugars 18.5g; Protein 4.7 g; Vitamin A 42%; Vitamin C 33%; Calcium 5%; Iron 16%

Green Vegetable Smoothie

Serves 2

1 cucumber

1 cup kale

2 stalks celery

1 stem broccoli

1 green apple

½ lemon, juiced

Nutrition Facts: Serving Size 336g; Calories 104; Calories from Fat 5; Total Fat 0.6g 1% DV; Cholesterol 0mg; Sodium 46mg 2% DV; Total Carbohydrates 24.8g 8% DV; Dietary Fiber 5.0 g 20% DV; Sugars 10.5; Protein 3.5g; Vitamin A 114%; Vitamin C 147%; Calcium 10%; Iron 8%

Strawberry and Rhubarb Smoothies

Strawberry Rhubarb Lemonade Slushy

This is a low calorie, no fat drink. Although it takes a little preparation, it will leave you feeling satisfied.

Serves 6

3 cups water

1 Rhubarb, chopped

2 lemons zested and juiced

3 cups strawberries, diced

Handful of ice

In a sauce pan combine water, rhubarb and lemon zest. Boil together for 15 minutes. Add strawberries and boil for 3 more minutes. Cool completely and blend. Add lemon juice and ice and blend until smooth.

Nutrition Facts: Serving size 381g; Calories 49; Calories from Fat 0; Total Fat 0.0g; Cholesterol 0mg; Sodium 7mg; Total Carbohydrates 10.8g 4% DV; Dietary Fiber 2.0g 8% DV; Sugars 7.8g; Protein 1.0g; Vitamin A 0%; Vitamin C 157%; Calcium 3%; Iron 2%

Strawberry Rhubarb Smoothie

Serves 2

1 ½ cup frozen strawberries

1 ½ cup rhubarb, chopped

1 ½ Tablespoon Raw Honey

2 cups almond milk

Blend all the ingredients together. Add more Honey if more sweetness is desired.

Nutrition Facts: Serving Size 321g; Calories 165; Calories from Fat 24; Total Fat 2.7g 4% DV; Cholesterol 0mg; Sodium 154mg 6% DV; Total Carbohydrates 34.9g 12% DV; Dietary Fiber 4.9g 20% DV; Sugars 27.6g; Protein 1.9g; Vitamin A 12%; Vitamin C 80%; Calcium 39%; Iron 7%

Spinach and Cucumber Smoothies

Cucumber Lime Smoothie

Serves 1

Enjoy this delicious, savory smoothie with more than your daily value of Vitamin A and Vitamin C.

½ cup Water

½ lime, juiced

¼ cup Ice

2/3 cup Red Bell Pepper

1 cup peeled Cucumber

1 cup Spinach

Pinch of Sea Salt

Nutrition Facts: Serving size 270g; Calories 26; Calories from Fat 3; Total Fat 0.3g 0% DV; Cholesterol 0mg; Sodium 265mg 11% DV; Total Carbohydrates 4.8g 2% DV; Dietary Fiber 2.0g 8% DV; Sugars 2.7g; Protein 1.5g; Vitamin A 95%; Vitamin C 145%; Calcium 4%; Iron 6%

Lemon Cucumber smoothie

Serves 1

1 Tablespoon Lemon Juice

1 Tablespoon Lime Juice

1 Cup Cucumber, Peeled

1 Tablespoon Avocado

Handful of Spinach

Sea Salt

Black Pepper

Handful of Ice

Add all the ingredients to a blender. Blend until smooth. Add salt and pepper to taste. The salt and pepper will soften the bite from the lemons and limes.

Nutrition Facts: Serving Size 128g; Calories 37; Calories from Fat 18; Total Fat 2.0g 3% DV; Cholesterol 0mg; Sodium 6mg 0% DV; Total Carbohydrates 4.1g 1% DV; Dietary Fiber 1.2g 5% DV; Protein 1.0g; Vitamin A 3%; Vitamin C 18%; Calcium 2%; Iron 2%

Coconut and Pineapple Smoothies

Pina Colada Smoothie

Serves 1

1 cup pineapple

1 fresh squeezed lime
1 banana
Ice cubes

Nutrition Facts: Serving Size 446g; Calories 244; Calories from Fat 6; Total Fat 0.7g 1% DV; Cholesterol 0mg; Sodium 5mg; Total Carbohydrates 64.1g 21% DV; Dietary Fiber 5.5g 22% DV; Sugars 38.7g; Protein 3.2g; Vitamin A 5%; Vitamin C 119%; Calcium 5%; Iron 6%

Spiced Pineapple Smoothie

Serves 2

1 Banana

1 ½ cups Pineapple

1 Orange

One Lime, juiced

1 Tablespoon ginger

½ teaspoon nutmeg

2 teaspoons turmeric

½ cup coconut milk

¾ cup water

Nutrition Facts: Serving Size 305g; Calories 254; Calories from Fat 137; Total Fat 15.2 23% DV; Saturated Fat 13.0g 65% DV; Cholesterol 0mg; Sodium 14mg 1% DV; Total Carbohydrates 31.2g 10% DV; Dietary Fiber 6.0g 24% DV; Sugars 18.1g; Protein 3.3g; Vitamin A 5%; Vitamin C 94%; Calcium 6%; Iron 14%

Pineapple Surprise Smoothie

Serves 3

1 avocado

1 ½ cups pineapple

1 egg yolk

1 ½ cup coconut milk

2 teaspoons lime juice

Ice cubes

Puree all the ingredients in the blender until smooth. Add ice until desired consistency.

Nutrition Facts: Serving Size 310g; Calories 474; Calories from Fat 390; Total Fat 43.3g 67% DV; Saturated Fat 27.3g 137% DV; Cholesterol 70mg 23% DV; Sodium 27mg 1% DV; Total Carbohydrates 20.7g 7% DV; Dietary Fiber 8.5g 34% DV; Sugars 12.7g; Protein 5.7g; Vitamin A 5%; Vitamin C 54%; Calcium 5%; Iron 16%

Lemon Detox Smoothies

Lemon- Lime Smoothie

Serves 2

½ Lemon, juiced

½ Lime, juiced

2 bananas

1 Orange, juiced

2 cups kale

Nutrition Facts: Serving Size 277g; Calories 182; Calories from Fat 9; Total Fat 1.0g 1% DV; Cholesterol 0mg; Sodium 30mg 1% DV; Total Carbohydrates 44.5g 15% DV; Dietary Fiber 6.6g 26% DV; Sugars 23.0g; Protein 4.4g; Vitamin A 212%; Vitamin C 233%; Calcium 13%; Iron 9%

Lemon, Mango Smoothie

Serves 1

½ lemon, juiced

1 mango, peeled and sliced

½ apple, peeled and sliced

2 cups spinach

½ cup water

Nutrition Facts: Serving Size 416g; Calories 213; Calories from Fat 13; Total Fat 1.4g 2% DV; Cholesterol 0mg; Sodium 53mg 2% DV; Total Carbohydrates 55.2g 18% DV; Dietary Fiber 9.1g 36% DV; Sugars 42.2g; Protein3.4g; Vitamin A 146%; Vitamin C 182%; Calcium 10%; Iron 13%

Pineapple, Lemon detox smoothie

Serves 1

1 cup fresh pineapple

½ lemon, juiced

1 cup spinach

¼ teaspoon fresh grated ginger

Nutrition Facts: Serving Size 343g; Calories 145; Calories from fat 5; Total Fat 0.5g 1% DV; Cholesterol 0mg; Sodium 27mg 1% DV; Total Carbohydrates 37.6g 13% DV; Dietary Fiber 3.8g 15% DV; Sugars 24.4g; Protein 2.9g; Vitamin A 59%; Vitamin C 120%; Calcium 7%; Iron 10%

Why Detox?

In today's world, our bodies are exposed to a multitude of toxins; pollution, chemicals in food, cleaning products, make-up and hair care products. Although our bodies are designed to get rid of these toxins it is exposed to, sometimes if the body is exposed to too many toxins, the body can't keep up.

There are several detox programs that one can follow. On average you need to detox for 7 days. The diet usually requires that you eat only raw fruits and vegetables for the duration of the diet.

Many claim that after a detox diet, they feel an increase of energy, they lose weight and overall they feel better.

Apple, Lemon Detox Smoothie

Serves 2

1 apple, with peel

1 lemon, juiced

1 cup kale

1 stalk of celery

1/3 cup fresh parsley

1 tablespoon chia seeds

¼ teaspoon cinnamon

1 cup water

Combine all the ingredients in a blender and blend until smooth.

Nutrition Facts: Serving size 22g; Calories 156; Calories from Fat 47; Total Fat 5.2g 8% DV; Saturated Fat 0.7g 3% DV; Cholesterol 0mg; Sodium 28mg 1% DV; Total Carbohydrates 25.0g 8% DV; Dietary Fiber 9.5g 38% DV; Sugars 10.4g; Protein 5.0g; Vitamin A 122%; Vitamin C 122%; Calcium 23%; Iron 21%

Tropical Fruit Smoothies

Papaya Smoothie

Serves 1

1 cup papaya

1 cup coconut milk

½ lime, juiced

1 Tablespoon raw honey

Nutrition Facts: Serving Size 401g; Calories 670; Calories from Fat 517; Total Fat 57.4g 88% DV; Saturated Fat 50.8g 254% DV; Cholesterol 0mg; Sodium 41mg 2% DV; Total Carbohydrates 44.3g 15% DV; Dietary Fiber 7.8g 31% DV; Sugars 33.5g; Protein 6.4g; Vitamin A 31%; Vitamin C 156%; Calcium 7%; Iron 23%